FACT or FICTION?

# DO UNICORNS EXIST?

PETER FINN

Gareth Stevens PUBLISHING

**Please visit our website, www.garethstevens.com. For a free color catalog of all our high-quality books, call toll free 1-800-542-2595 or fax 1-877-542-2596.**

**Library of Congress Cataloging-in-Publication Data**

Names: Finn, Peter, 1978- author.
Title: Do unicorns exist? / Peter Finn.
Description: New York: Gareth Stevens Publishing, [2023] | Series: Fact or fiction? | Includes index.
Identifiers: LCCN 2021059685 (print) | LCCN 2021059686 (ebook) | ISBN 9781538280898 (Library Binding) | ISBN 9781538280874 (Paperback) | ISBN 9781538280881 (Set) | ISBN 9781538280904 (eBook)
Subjects: LCSH: Unicorns–Juvenile literature. | Unicorns–Folklore–Juvenile literature.
Classification: LCC GR830.U6 F56 2023 (print) | LCC GR830.U6 (ebook) | DDC 398.24/54–dc23/eng/20220126
LC record available at https://lccn.loc.gov/2021059685
LC ebook record available at https://lccn.loc.gov/2021059686

Published in 2023 by
**Gareth Stevens Publishing**
29 E. 21st Street
New York, NY 10010



Designer: Sheryl Kober
Editor: Therese Shea

Photo credits: Cover (top) and p. 1 funstarts33/Shutterstock.com; cover and p. 1 (middle glitter texture) Valentina Azhgirevich/Shutterstock.com; cover and p. 1 (bottom image) New Africa/Shutterstock.com; pp. 1–32 (sky background texture) New Africa/Shutterstock.com; pp. 1–32 (heading and sidebar background) Valentina Azhgirevich /Shutterstock.com; back cover and pp. 2–32 (It's A Fact background texture) CARACOLLA/Shutterstock.com; p. 3 (unicorn bottom) New Africa/Shutterstock.com; p. 4 sufi23/Shutterstock.com; p. 5 (top) T Studio/Shutterstock.com; p. 5 (bottom) warasit phothisuk/Shutterstock.com; p. 6 Barashkova Natalia/Shutterstock.com; p. 7 (top) Solomandra/Shutterstock.com; p. 7 (bottom) paseven/Shutterstock.com; p. 8 Morphart Creation/Shutterstock.com; p. 9 (top) Lewis Liu/Shutterstock.com; p. 9 (bottom) paseven/Shutterstock.com; p. 10 A.Sych/Shutterstock.com; p. 11 (top) Paco Como/Shutterstock.com; p. 11 (bottom) RudiErnst/Shutterstock.com; p. 12 BlueLotusArt/Shutterstock.com; p. 13 (top left) https://en.wikipedia.org/wiki/Al-Mi%27raj#/media/File:Al-miraj_and_Serpent.png; p. 13 (top right) https://en.wikipedia.org/wiki/Al-Mi%27raj#/media/File:Al-miraj_and_Serpent.png; p. 13 (bottom) Drawlab19/Shutterstock.com; p. 14 Wonder-studio/Shutterstock.com; p. 15 (top) https://en.wikipedia.org/wiki/Great_Moon_Hoax#/media/File:Great-Moon-Hoax-1835-New-York-Sun-lithograph-298px.jpg; p. 15 (middle) https://en.wikipedia.org/wiki/Bestiary#/media/File:85-Oxford_1511_-_Unicorno.jpg; p. 15 (bottom) New Africa/Shutterstock.com; p. 16 OlgaChernyak/Shutterstock.com; p. 17 (top) Dotted Yeti/Shutterstock.com; p. 17 (bottom) DAndrea Izzotti/Shutterstock.com; p. 18 Vera Petruk/Shutterstock.com; p. 19 (The Unicorn Tapestries, top left to bottom right) The Metropolitan Museum of Art, New York. Gift of John D. Rockefeller Jr., 1937 www.metmuseum.org; p. 20 (top) Verko_o/Shutterstock.com; p. 20 (bottom) Liliya Butenko/Shutterstock.com; p. 21 (top) Tehrlif/Shutterstock.com; p. 21 (parchment background) Nella/Shutterstock.com; p. 21 (unicorn, bottom) Tateshi/Shutterstock.com; p. 22 Morphart Creation/Shutterstock.com; p. 23 (top) Nityanand Nawalkar/Shutterstock.com; p. 23 (bottom) Katiekk/Shutterstock.com; p. 24 (top) Alex Rockheart/Shutterstock.com; p. 24 (bottom) https://en.wikipedia.org/wiki/Elasmotherium#/media/File:Elasm062.jpg; p. 25 (top) Dotted Yeti/Shutterstock.com; p. 25 (bottom) Morphart Cration/Shutterstock.com; p. 26 (top) Alexander_P/Shutterstock.com; p. 26 (bottom) Andrey Shcherbukin/Shutterstock.com; p. 27 (top) Olena Piatenko/Shutterstock.com; p. 27 (bottom) Siarhei Bezpalka/Shutterstock.com; p. 28 pixpenart/Shutterstock.com; p. 29 (top) Stacey Ann Alberts/Shutterstock.com; p. 29 (middle) Martin Prochazkacz/Shutterstock.com; p. 29 (bottom) Jane Rix/Shutterstock.com



Printed in the United States of America

CPSIA compliance information: Batch #CSGS23: For further information contact Gareth Stevens, New York, New York, at 1-800-542-2595.

# Contents

Words in the glossary appear in **bold** type the first time they are used in the text.

# A Single Horn

Imagine taking a walk in the woods. Suddenly, you notice a large white animal through the trees. It's bent down, drinking from a stream. As you get closer, you see it has the body of a horse. It raises its head, and you spot a single horn sticking out of its forehead. It's a unicorn! Next, you might find a camera and take a picture as quickly as you can. An **authentic** photo would turn this creature from legend to actual animal.

While stories about unicorns have been passed down over centuries, they've never been proven to be true. Is it fair to label unicorns as a myth just because they've never been photographed or captured? Let's learn more about them before deciding if they could exist.

## THE U.K. AND THE UNICORN

The unicorn is on the **coat of arms** of the British queen, Elizabeth II. The legendary animal is a symbol of Scotland, while the lion represents England. In the coat of arms, these animals are depicted, or shown, supporting a shield between them with more symbols within the shield representing England, Scotland, and Ireland. The unicorn is a common decoration in Great Britain. It's found on the front gates of Buckingham Palace, shown on the next page, the Queen's London home.

The word "unicorn" was first used in the 13th century. People have been talking about these creatures for a long time!

**IT'S A FACT!**

"Unicorn" comes from the Latin terms *uni-* and *cornu*, meaning "having one horn."

# Not So Strange?

Myths are filled with strange creatures. A sphinx has a human head and a lion's body. Centaurs have the lower body of a horse and the upper body of a man. A griffin has a lion's body and a bird's head, often an eagle's. It may or may not have wings. A hippogriff is part horse and part griffin. A phoenix is said to be a bird with red and gold feathers that sets itself on fire so another phoenix can be reborn from its ashes.

Compared to these legendary beasts, unicorns might not seem so strange. They're often described as horse-like, and sometimes goat-like, with a single long horn on their head. It wasn't hard for people in the past to believe in unicorns, even if they had never seen one.

## A MIX OF CHARACTERISTICS

Throughout history, people have told stories about unicorns. Reports of these creatures come from India, Africa, Asia, and Europe. In some tales, these animals are gentle, kind, and loving. In others, unicorns are fierce, strong, and fast. It's said they like to be alone and are almost impossible to catch, which helps explain why so few have seen them. Their coats have been described as different colors, though often white and sometimes reddish, and their horns are said to be various colors too.

**The myth of the griffin, also called a griffon or gryphon, may have been told as early as 2000 BCE!**

## IT'S A FACT!

In the 17th century, German scientist Otto von Guericke said animal bones found in a cave were a unicorn skeleton. They were actually the remains of a woolly rhinoceros.

# Unicorn Tales Around the World

Confucius

Ancient Chinese stories tell of a *qilin*, a unicorn-like creature, in the garden of Huangdi, the Yellow Emperor, in 2697 BCE. It had one horn on its head, a yellow stomach, a deer's body, and an ox's tail. The creature was so gentle that it didn't eat plants or even walk on grass. To the Chinese, its appearance meant the birth or death of a great person. One was said to have appeared before the birth of the philosopher Confucius in the sixth century BCE.

The Japanese also had unicorn legends. According to some tales, the creature could find criminals and punish them by plunging its horn into their hearts! The animal was called a *kirin*. This word also came to mean "giraffe" in Japanese.

## THE UNICORN OF LASCAUX

Lascaux is a cave in France that contains prehistoric art in the form of engravings, drawings, and painted figures. It's thought by some that the artwork, which includes mostly animals and symbols, may date back 15,000 to 17,000 years. One of the animals featured has two long, straight horns placed closely together. Despite the two horns, this beast, which hasn't been identified yet as another animal, is called the Lascaux unicorn.

*Qilin* are depicted in the Forbidden City, the imperial palace in Beijing, China.

IT'S A FACT!

The name for the constellation Monoceros (above) comes from a Greek word that means "unicorn."

Greek doctor Ctesias, who was born at the end of the fifth century BCE, traveled to Persia (today's Iran). While there, he heard travelers talking about strange, horse-like animals they had seen in India. These creatures, according to the travelers, had "a horn on the forehead, which is about a foot and a half [0.5 m] in length." The horn was white, black, and red. The animals were so fast that no other creatures could outrun them.

Pliny the Elder

More than 400 years later, Roman Pliny the Elder (23–79 CE) wrote many volumes to create his work called *Natural History.* This was a kind of encyclopedia that included legendary animals. In it, he described a unicorn, calling it a "monoceros" or "licorne." Pliny said it was a "furious beast."

## PLINY'S PORTRAYAL OF THE UNICORN

A 1634 translation of Pliny's *Natural History* includes text about unicorns. (Notice the different spellings of the time.) "But the most fell [fierce] and furious beast of all other, is the Licorne or Monoceros: his bodie [body] resembleth an horse, his head a stagge [stag], his feet an Elephant, his taile a bore [boar]; . . . one blacke horn he hath [has] in the mids [middle] of his forehead, . . . by report, this wild beast cannot possibly be caught alive."

Many people think both Ctesias and Pliny the Elder were describing one-horned rhinoceroses rather than unicorns.

**IT'S A FACT!**

Today, there are two species of one-horned rhinoceroses. They live in pockets of the northern part of the Indian **subcontinent** and the Southeast Asian island of Java.

In the 13th century, a Persian doctor, astronomer, and geographer named Abu Yahya Zakariya ibn Muhammad al-Qazwini wrote a book called, in English, *Marvels of Creation and Rarities of Existence.* While he described many animals proven to exist, he also gave details of legendary creatures, including *al-mi'raj*. It was said to look like a large rabbit with a horn coming out of its forehead. *Al-mi'raj*, or the mi'raj, was supposedly so fierce that other wild animals ran away from it. *Al-mi'raj* was said to live only on an island in the Indian Ocean, but was gifted to Alexander the Great (356–323 BCE).

The *karkadann* was another legendary one-horned animal, which was also said to be fearsome. Al-Qazwini claimed its horn had medicinal qualities and could even serve as an **antidote** to poison.

## LOST IN TRANSLATION?

The Old Testament of the Bible was translated from Hebrew into Greek in the third century BCE. The Hebrew text told of a large, powerful animal with a horn, called a *re'em*, the word for a wild ox. This was translated into Greek as *monokeros*, which means "one-horned beast." Later, the word was translated into Latin as *unicornus* and then into the English "unicorn." Many people believed in unicorns because they were written about in early Bibles.

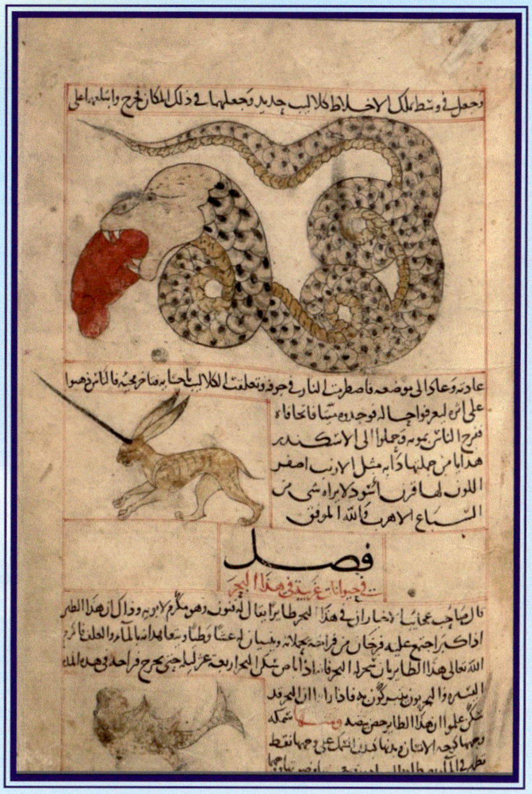

Al-Qazwini's *Marvels of Creation and Rarities of Existence* was widely read, which spread the legend of unicorn-like creatures.

**IT'S A FACT!**

In religious artwork, the unicorn often represents Jesus Christ.

# Through the Middle Ages

Works like al-Qazwini's are sometimes called bestiaries. Bestiaries were like an encyclopedia of animals, plants, and even stones. **Medieval** bestiaries spread the belief in unicorns. Much of the information in some bestiaries came from a second-century Greek text—and not all the "facts" were true. Ideas from ancient historians such as Pliny the Elder were also featured. Some entries were presented more like stories, often with a religious moral. Unicorns, phoenixes, and centaurs were included, aiding in keeping alive the legend of unicorns and other mythical animals.

But at the end of the Middle Ages, doubts about the existence of unicorns had emerged. As explorers reached far points around the globe, people realized unicorns hadn't been seen. There were fewer and fewer unexplored places left where such an animal could live.

## ON THE MOON?

In 1835, articles began appearing in the *New York Sun* newspaper that announced life had been discovered on the moon. The writer said the discovery came from real-life astronomer Sir John Herschel, who was, in fact, using a new telescope with greater power. The writer said Herschel found proof that animals, including unicorns, were living on the moon. Weeks later, the *Sun* admitted the articles, which helped sell many newspapers, weren't true.

The image above depicts the *New York Sun* hoax of 1835. It shows mythical moon animals, including unicorns.

Bestiary

**IT'S A FACT!**

In 1827, scientist Georges Cuvier said that a unicorn couldn't exist. He stated that such a horn wouldn't be able to grow in the center of an animal's skull.

# All About the Horn

The horn is what makes the unicorn special among legendary animals. It was thought to have special powers. In some stories and art, the creature used its horn to make unclean waters pure. Cups said to be made of unicorn horns were believed to purify the liquids within them. Unicorn horns were also thought to be able to cure plague in the Middle Ages as well as many other disorders and diseases.

Because unicorns were said to be so hard to catch, horns sold at a high price. Queen Elizabeth I (1533–1603) of England was said to own a horn worth the price of a castle! But what were people using if not actual unicorn horns? The tusks of the medium-sized whales called narwhals were often sold as unicorn horns.

## MAKING MEDICINES

An apothecary is someone who prepares and sells drugs used as medicines. This term has been largely replaced with "pharmacist." Medieval apothecaries made medicine, too, sometimes telling customers they put ground unicorn horns in their mixtures. Although they often used narwhal tusk, sometimes they used tusks of other animals including elephants and walruses as well. At times, even the apothecaries had no idea what animal the matter came from!

Narwhal tusks became more valuable than gold because of the belief in unicorn horns' magical and healing properties.

IT'S A FACT!

Another name for a unicorn horn is an alicorn.

# Catching a Unicorn

Most unicorn tales describe the animals as nearly impossible to capture. They were said to be so swift they could easily outrun hunters. That was a good reason why there was so little proof of their existence. They also had a deadly weapon on their head, their horn, which was said to be able to kill elephants. But some storytellers offered hints about how to catch these beasts.

First, they said, find the forest or habitat where the unicorn has been seen. Next, ask for the help of a young girl. (Girls are known to attract unicorns. The creatures settle down and may even put their heads in a girl's lap.) Seat the young girl in a clearing, while hunters are hidden nearby. When the unicorn approaches the girl, the hunters can strike.

## THE UNICORN TAPESTRIES

Seven **tapestries** from France are considered some of the greatest medieval artwork. Woven with wool, silk, silver, and gold threads, these "Unicorn Tapestries" feature the story of a unicorn hunt. Over the years, the tapestries—created between 1495 and 1505—were stolen, hidden away, rediscovered, and finally transported to the United States. They were donated to the Metropolitan Museum of Art in New York City, where they can be viewed at the branch called the Cloisters.

# The Unicorn Tapestries

*The Hunters Enter the Woods*

*The Unicorn Purifies Water*

*The Unicorn Crosses a Stream*

*The Unicorn Defends Himself*

*The Unicorn Surrenders to a Maiden*

*The Hunters Return to the Castle*

*The Unicorn Rests in a Garden*

**The tapestry called *The Unicorn Rests in a Garden* may not have been created to accompany the rest of this series. Others think it shows the unicorn following the hunt, after it came back to life.**

**IT'S A FACT!**

At one point, the Unicorn Tapestries were used to wrap fruit trees in winter.

The interest in hunting unicorns hasn't died out, even though many people don't believe in them anymore. In fact, a university in Michigan issues licenses to hunt them! In the 1970s, the Department of Natural Unicorns of the Unicorn Hunters was formed at Lake Superior State University. ("Hunting" licenses were later changed to "questing" licenses so that the school didn't appear to be encouraging the killing of unicorns.)

According to this department, unicorn questers may use bows and rubber-tipped arrows only during the first week of October. They can hunt for unicorns using other methods any day except for Valentine's Day and "when the Tooth Fairy or Santa Claus is around." The department also suggests where to find unicorns: "enchanted forests, Earth, outer space, [and your] imagination."

## ARTHURIAN LEGENDS

Among the books that the Department of Natural Unicorns recommends unicorn questers take with them are Arthurian legends. These are tales of the legendary King Arthur, who was said to have ruled ancient Britain, and his knights. In the stories, some of which were told earlier than the 12th century, Arthur and his knights encountered many mythical beasts. In one story, the heart of a unicorn (or "monocerous") is used to try to heal a king.

The Department of Natural Unicorns at Lake Superior State University recommends bringing items for a unicorn quest, such as:

*serious focus*
*lightheartedness*
*flattery*
*drinks for questers and potions for unicorns*
*horse comb*
*nail clipper*
*horn and hoof trimmer*
*horn and hoof polish*
*ribbons*
*Arthurian legends*

**IT'S A FACT!**

Lake Superior State University's Department of Natural Unicorns still issues free unicorn questing licenses.

# Looking in Nature

If unicorns weren't real, where did tales about them come from? And what made unicorn tales so common in **cultures** around the globe? It may be that the legend comes from animals that we know exist.

For example, an oryx is a type of antelope that lives in Africa and on the Arabian **peninsula**. It has two long, straight horns. If travelers spotted an oryx from the side or from far away, they might have thought it had one horn instead of two—just like a unicorn!

In the 13th century, Italian explorer Marco Polo said he saw unicorns on the Southeast Asian island of Sumatra, but some think he actually saw rhinoceroses. He remarked that they were ugly and as big as elephants. But since they had one horn, he assumed they were unicorns.

## MARCO POLO'S INCREDIBLE TALES

Marco Polo (about 1254–1324) traveled through China and other parts of Asia. He saw and experienced things that Europeans hadn't heard of yet. Some of the tales he returned to Italy with are based in fact, such as black stones that burned like logs (or coal). But other parts are **exaggerations** or entirely imagined. For example, he said he saw in Sumatra "men who have tails more than a palm in size."

Perhaps people saw an oryx (right), rhinoceros (above), or similar creature from a distance and mistook it for a unicorn.

**IT'S A FACT!**

Marco Polo described his travels in a book called *Il milione* (*The Million*). It's often called *Travels of Marco Polo* in English.

While a narwhal's body doesn't resemble a unicorn's body as we think of it, its tusk does look like a unicorn's horn. The narwhal, sometimes called a narwhale, lives in Arctic waters. It usually doesn't grow to be more than 17 feet (5.2 m) long. The tusk, which is a tooth, can be 10 feet (3 m) long. Some narwhals have two tusks, some have one, and some don't have any. The tusk develops with a **spiraling** groove.

There are a few theories about why narwhals have tusks. It may have to do with males competing for mates, though some females have tusks. It may have to do with hunting, though they don't use tusks to spear food. Instead, they give prey a quick tap to stun it.

## ANCIENT UNICORN

It's possible that an animal that no longer exists inspired the unicorn legend. One candidate is the *Elasmotherium sibiricum*, also known as the Siberian unicorn. This rhinoceros species likely died out over 35,000 years ago. While fossils of this animal have been uncovered, no horn has been yet. Still, scientists believe it had one large horn on its head. Humans who lived at the same time as the rhinoceros may have passed down stories of the fierce, one-horned creature.

A narwhal tusk has 10 million nerve endings inside it! These may help a narwhal sense changes in the water.

IT'S A FACT!

A narwhal has two teeth, both in its upper jaw. In males, usually just the left tooth grows into a tusk. Some females have a tusk, though. Rarely, both teeth develop into tusks in narwhals.

# Unicorns Today

You probably won't be surprised to read that the unicorn legend hasn't died out. Unicorns are in books, songs, movies, and television shows. They're in games and on clothing, blankets, pillows, and so much more. Unlike the unicorns of old tales, unicorns today are often brightly colored and appear quite gentle. While they certainly appeal to young people, there are plenty of older unicorn buffs too.

If you're a fan of Pokémon games, you've definitely seen a few unicorn characters. One-horned horses are a part of the *My Little Pony* TV series too. People who read the Harry Potter book series and watch the movies know that some wands have a single unicorn hair at their center, providing them with magic.

## A UNICORN THRONE?

**The unicorn is a symbol of royalty in countries other than England and Scotland. In Denmark, parts of a royal throne were said to be made of unicorn horns! Created in the 1600s, the Throne Chair of Denmark has legs and spokes with a spiraling pattern that look like unicorn horns. They're actually made out of narwhal tusks, however. This throne is no longer used for official royal activities in Denmark.**

Some people think unicorns remain a part of popular culture because they remind people of their childhood.

**IT'S A FACT!**

In 2010, a birdwatcher gave the Ontario Science Centre in Canada a video of a unicorn. However, the video was found to be a hoax.

# What Do You Believe?

Maybe unicorns did exist at one time. After all, many species of strange creatures on Earth have gone extinct. There are also animals born a bit different than the rest of their species. In 2008, a one-horned deer was spotted in a wildlife preserve in Italy. Scientists believe the single horn is the result of a **gene mutation**.

Some animals may sound unbelievable if you didn't know they existed. Think about the length of a giraffe's neck, the **flexibility** of an elephant's trunk, or the number of teeth a great white shark can grow in a lifetime (50,000!). Certainly, if you couldn't see these creatures, you might think they couldn't possibly be real. So, what do you think about unicorns? Could they be real?

## LANCELOT THE UNICORN

In 1985, the Ringling Bros. and Barnum & Bailey Circus announced it had a unicorn as part of its acts. People went to see the one-horned animal, named Lancelot, and wondered how it grew this horn. Animal rights organizations worried the animal, a goat, had been mistreated in some way. An **x-ray** revealed the horn was natural. However, the goat's horn buds had been stitched together so they grew as one in the center of its head.

A lot of animals that we know exist have extraordinary features. Can you think of other creatures with odd body parts or remarkable behaviors?

IT'S A FACT!

"Unicorn" is also a word for a new business that's worth more than $1 billion.

# Glossary

**antidote:** something used to stop the effects of a poison

**authentic:** shown to be true and trustworthy

**coat of arms:** a design of symbols standing for a family, city, or country

**culture:** the beliefs and ways of life of a group of people

**exaggeration:** the act of thinking of or describing something as larger or greater than it really is

**flexibility:** having the ability to bend easily without breaking

**gene mutation:** a permanent change in a gene that may or may not have an effect on the body

**medieval:** having to do with the Middle Ages, a time in European history from about 500 to 1500

**peninsula:** a narrow piece of land that extends into water from the mainland

**spiraling:** curling outward from a center point or inward towards a center point

**subcontinent:** a large landmass that is a part of a continent

**tapestry:** a heavy reversible cloth woven by hand that often has pictures or designs on it

**x-ray:** a powerful type of energy that is similar to light but is invisible to the human eye

# For More Information

## BOOKS

Alberti, Theresa Jarosz. *Unicorns.* New York, NY: AV2 by Weigl, 2020.

Loh-Hagan, Virginia. *Unicorns: Magic, Myth, and Mystery.* Ann Arbor, MI: Cherry Lake Publishing, 2017.

Phipps, Selwyn E. *The Magical Unicorn Society: A Brief History of Unicorns.* New York, NY: Feiwel and Friends, 2019.

## WEBSITES

### Are Unicorns Real?

*wonderopolis.org/wonder/are-unicorns-real*

Read how real animals may have inspired the legend of the unicorn.

### Unicorns, West and East

*www.amnh.org/exhibitions/mythic-creatures/land/unicorns-west-and-east*

The American Museum of Natural History has collected stories and myths of unicorns.

**Publisher's note to educators and parents:** Our editors have carefully reviewed these websites to ensure that they are suitable for students. Many websites change frequently, however, and we cannot guarantee that a site's future contents will continue to meet our high standards and educational value. Be advised that students should be clearly supervised whenever they access the internet.

# Index